Too Broke For Bankruptcy

The Step-by-Step Guide to Filing Bankruptcy Without an Attorney

Nic Jones

Copyright © 2018 by Nic Jones
All rights reserved. This book or any portion thereof may not be reproduced or used in any manner without the express written permission of the publisher, except for the use of brief quotations in a book review.

This book is not intended to substitute legal advice. Although the author and publisher have made every effort to ensure that the information in this book was correct at press time, the author and publisher do not assume and hereby disclaim any liability to any party for any loss, damage, or disruption caused by errors or omissions, whether such errors or omissions result from negligence, accident, or any other cause.

Table of Contents

Introduction 1
Who Is Eligible to File Chapter 7 Bankruptcy? 3
    The "Means Test" 3
    Means Test Part 2 5
What Type of Debt Can be Discharged? 7
    Non-Dischargeable Debt 7
    Common Dischargeable Debt 8
    Presumption of Fraud 8
What Assets & Property Are Exempt? 10
What Options Are There For Secured Property? 11
    Reaffirming Secured Property 11
    Reaffirming Credit Union Debt 12
    Redeeming Secured Property 13
    Surrendering Secured Property 13
Pre-Bankruptcy Tasks 14
    Task 1: Consider Switching Banks or Credit Unions 14
    Task 2: Determine the Value of Your Assets 14
    Task 3: Complete the Required Credit Counseling 15
Filing Chapter 7 Bankruptcy 16
    Step 1: Decide How You'll Pay the Filing Fee 16
    Step 2: Complete a Creditor Matrix 17
    Step 3: Complete the Required Forms 18
    Step 4: Attend the Meeting of Creditors 22
    Step 5: Complete the Required Debtor Education Course ... 23
Discharge and Beyond 24
Glossary for Chapter 7 Bankruptcy 25

Introduction

Too broke for bankruptcy. It sounds like a bad joke, but it isn't.

Making the decision to file Chapter 7 bankruptcy isn't easy. Bankruptcy, unfortunately, has a negative stigma and many people considering filing see it as a sign of failure. I'm here to tell you that it's not. Sure, the decision to file bankruptcy shouldn't be taken lightly and it *will* have some impact on your credit score. But bankruptcy is also a chance for a fresh start.

Do you know what's even more difficult than deciding to file? Figuring out how to pay for it. Especially when a lot of attorneys charge between upwards of $1,500. I don't know about you, but when I was ready to file bankruptcy it was because I was **broke**. I didn't have any money to put towards an attorney. I almost put off filing until I could afford an attorney, but then I realized how easy it was to file without an attorney.

When you're at rock bottom, taking a do-it-yourself approach to filing bankruptcy may be your only option for filing bankruptcy. It was for me at least, and it is for many others too. With the right preparation and understanding of the various bankruptcy codes, filing "pro se" might be right for you too.

Whether or not you should file bankruptcy without an attorney really depends on your financial situation, the types of debt you have, and your assets. The complexity of your case matters and sometimes, hiring an attorney really is your best option. If your case is pretty straight forward, however, filing Chapter 7 bankruptcy alone is entirely possible.

Chapter 7 bankruptcy is the most common type of bankruptcy and it allows you to discharge most of your debts. Unlike Chapter 13 bankruptcy, you don't need to develop a repayment plan. By "liquidating" your non-exempt assets, you can get rid of most of your debt and wipe the slate clean, so to speak.

In Chapter 7 bankruptcy, most unsecured debts such as medical bills, personal loans, and credit cards are forgiven. You also have the option to seek reaffirmation on secured debts, such as automobile loans and mortgages. There are, however, some types of debt you cannot discharge. This includes child support, property taxes, etc.

In this book, you'll learn more about the types of debts you can discharge in bankruptcy and the basics of reaffirming debt. You will also learn who qualifies for Chapter 7 bankruptcy and what types of debt can be discharged. *Too Broke For Bankruptcy* is your guide for filing bankruptcy on your own.

Who Is Eligible to File Chapter 7 Bankruptcy?

When it comes to filing Chapter 7 bankruptcy, there are several factors to consider. This includes your income, ability to repay debt, bankruptcy history, and whether or not fraud is suspected.

The "Means Test"

The means test will determine whether or not you qualify for Chapter 7 bankruptcy. If your income is too high, the court may decide to convert your case to a Chapter 13 bankruptcy and a repayment plan will be implemented.

The means test is two parts:

1: Is your income equal to or below your state's median income? If it is, you qualify to file Chapter 7 bankruptcy.

2. If your income is higher than your state's median income, is your disposable income high enough to repay unsecured creditors through a Chapter 13 repayment plan?

Means Test Part 1

When comparing your income to your state's median income, your household size is important. For most, this is easy to determine. If you have unusual living arrangements, however, it can be more challenging to accurately determine your household size. Most courts allow you to count all people who occupy a housing unit as their usual place of residence. Some, however, require you to claim the household member as a dependent on your taxes.

If you're not sure whether or not someone qualifies as a household member, first take the means test without counting them as a household member. If you qualify, great! If not, run it again using the household member. If counting that person qualifies you, it might be a good idea to consult an attorney to see whether or not they can be included as a household member.

Calculating Current Monthly Income (CMI)
Once you know your household size, calculate your current monthly income (CMI). This is an average of the income you've received in the six months period before you file bankruptcy. To get the CMI, add your total income over the six months and then divide by six.

This income must include:
- Your gross wages (including overtime) or salary.
- Bonuses, tips, and commissions.
- Business or professional income.
- Any interest, dividends, or royalties you receive.
- Annuity payments.
- Rental income.
- Regular child support or spousal support payments.
- Unemployment or workers' compensation payments.
- Pension or retirement income.
- State disability insurance payments.
- Veterans' benefits.

Some types of income are excluded. You don't need to count:
- Social Security retirement income.
- SSI or SSDI payments.
- TANF payments.

If you are considered a disabled veteran, you are exempt from the means test if you incurred the debt while on active duty or performing a homeland defense activity **and**:
- You are rated by the Veterans Administration as at least 30% disabled, or
- You are discharged as a result of a disability incurred in the line of duty.

Comparing Your Income to Your State Median Income
Once you calculate your CMI, multiple it by 12 to calculate your annual income. Compare this figure to the median family income for your state listed at: https://www.justice.gov/ust/means-testing

If your income is at or below the median income for your household size, you've passed the means test. If not, continue to take part two of the means test.

Means Test Part 2

If your income is above your state's median income, you'll need to complete the Chapter 7 Means Test Calculation (Form 122A-2): http://www.uscourts.gov/forms/means-test-forms/chapter-7-means-test-calculation. This form will compare your CMI to your allowable expenses to determine your disposable income. These expenses include things, such as medical costs, rent, groceries, etc.

Too Broke For Bankruptcy

If your disposable income is low enough, you qualify for Chapter 7 bankruptcy. If your disposable income is too high, there is a presumption of abuse. If there are special circumstances, such as a recent divorce or separation, you can continue to file Chapter 7 bankruptcy by completing part 4 of the form and the court will decide whether or not you qualify.

What Type of Debt Can be Discharged?

The nice thing about Chapter 7 bankruptcy is that most unsecured debt can be discharged. A discharge protects you from personal liability for the debt and prevents your creditors from taking collection or legal action against you for the debt.

Non-Dischargeable Debt
Some types of debt are always considered non-dischargeable. Unless you can show you have extraordinary circumstances, these debts are typically non-dischargeable:
- Debts you don't list on the bankruptcy petition or include on the mailing list unless the creditor had actual notice or knowledge of the bankruptcy filing.
- Child support, spousal support, or alimony debts.
- Debts for personal injury caused by a DUI or DWI.
- Fines and penalties owed to government agencies.
- Student loans.
- Some tax debts.
- Debts owed to a former spouse or child from a divorce or separation.
- debts owed to certain tax-advantaged retirement plans
- Homeowners association fees and similar debts.
- Attorney fees in child custody and support cases.
- Court fines, penalties, and restitution.

If you owe these types of debts or believe you have extraordinary circumstances, consider consulting with an attorney before filing bankruptcy.

Common Dischargeable Debt

Debt that doesn't meet any of the above categories is considered a dischargeable debt. Some examples include:
- Credit card debt.
- Medical bills (current and past due).
- Collection agency accounts.
- Past due utility bills.
- NSF checks (unless it is fraud-related).
- Personal loans.
- Loans from family and friends.
- Non-DUI automobile accident claims.
- Store credit cards
- Civil court judgements (unless it is fraud-related).
- Veterans overpayments.
- Social security overpayments.

Presumption of Fraud

Although debt may be considered dischargeable, creditors can file a complaint and object to discharge if there is a presumption of fraud. The court will then hold a hearing to determine whether or not the debt is dischargeable. Below are debts that have the presumption of fraud.

Luxury Purchases Made Within 90 Days of Filing

If you spent more than $675 on credit from one creditor within 90 days of filing bankruptcy, the purchase(s) are presumed to be fraudulently made with no intent to pay. If you can prove to the court that the purchase wasn't for luxury items, you may still be able to get the debt discharged. Some non-luxury purchases may include gas, groceries, clothing, etc.

Cash Advances Taken Out Within 70 Days of Filing

If you took out cash advances totaling more than $950 from one creditor within 70 days of filing for bankruptcy, the debt isn't dischargeable. If for example, you took out $700 from one creditor and $400 from another, the debt isn't presumed to be fraudulent.

What Assets & Property Are Exempt?

One of the biggest myths about filing bankruptcy is that you'll lose everything. Don't worry, your trustee won't be coming to auction off everything you own. Most Chapter 7 bankruptcies filed are considered no-asset cases. This means the debtor doesn't have non-exempt property and there are no assets that can be sold to pay creditors.

The exemptions you qualify for will vary from state to state, however most offer a homestead exemption, vehicle exemption, and retirement account exemption. Wages are also often exempt and many states have a wildcard exemption allowing you to choose which assets to protect. No matter where you live, your clothing and household items are exempt, unless they are considered highly valuable.

When you file bankruptcy, you will list all of your assets (including exempt property) and their value on Schedule A/B: Property (Official Form 106A/B). Be sure you also list any exempt assets on Schedule C: The Property You Claim as Exempt (Official Form 106C). If you do not include an exempt asset on this form, the trustee may sell it and pay all of the proceeds to your creditors.

If you do have significant equity in your home or own vehicles free and clear, consulting with an attorney can help you determine which exemptions you can use.

What Options Are There For Secured Property?

When you have secured debts, such as mortgages and automobile loans, your creditor has the right to take the property (the collateral) if you don't pay on the debt. Once you file bankruptcy, an automatic stay (discussed more in Chapter X) prevents your creditor from repossessing,
foreclosing, or selling the secured property.

During bankruptcy, you'll need to decide whether you intend on reaffirming, redeeming, or surrendering the property. When you file bankruptcy, you'll state your intent on the Statement of Intention for Individuals Filing Under Chapter 7 (Official Form 108), however, this is not binding.

If you declare you intend to reaffirm a loan, you are under no obligation to complete a reaffirmation agreement. Likewise, many times debtors declare an intent to surrender the property and the creditor reaches out to request a reaffirmation agreement.

Reaffirming Secured Property

One option you have if reaffirming the debt. When you do this, you agree to remain responsible for the debt and make payments so you can keep the property. During the reaffirmation process, you may also have the opportunity to renegotiate terms of the agreement, such as the interest rate or payment amount. These agreements are voluntary and both you and your creditor must agree and sign the Form 240A Reaffirmation Agreement: http://www.uscourts.gov/sites/default/files/b_240a_0410.pdf

When you file bankruptcy without an attorney, any reaffirmation other than debt secured by real estate requires court approval. A hearing will be held and the court will determine whether or not the reaffirmation is in your best interest. If, for example, you owe $14,250 on a vehicle worth $8,600, the court may decide the reaffirmation is not in your best interest.

If you do intend on entering into a reaffirmation agreement, make sure you stay current on payments before filing bankruptcy. If you are behind on payments, your creditor may require you to pay the outstanding balance before they will agree to reaffirm the debt.

Note: You can cancel a reaffirmation at any time before your discharge or within 60 days from when the reaffirmation agreement is filed with the court.

Reaffirming Credit Union Debt

Reaffirming debt with credit unions doesn't require court approval. Once any reaffirmation agreements with a credit union are filed, they become part of the record without a hearing. If you intend to reaffirm secured debt with a credit union, it's wise to consult an attorney because of cross-collateralization.

Many loan agreements with credit unions contain a cross-collateralization clause. This means the property you are using as collateral for the loan can also be used as collateral for any and all debt you have with the credit union. When you file bankruptcy, if you want to reaffirm the secured loan, your credit union may also require you to reaffirm unsecured loans.

Redeeming Secured Property

Another option is to redeem. Redemption offers you a way to buy back your collateral from your creditor for the replacement value rather than what you actually owe. Once you redeem the property, you own it free and clear. This can be very beneficial if you owe significantly more than your property is worth and if you have the money available.

Redeeming is only allowed for personal, non-real estate property. The redemption value is the amount a retail merchant would charge for the property you have taking into account the age and condition of your property. If you and the creditor can't agree on the value, the court may hold a valuation hearing.

Surrendering Secured Property

Surrendering secured property is common. It is also the simplest way to handle secured debt and property. When you surrender secured property, you give the property back to your creditor and the debt is wiped out with bankruptcy. Surrendering secured property may be a good idea if you no longer want the property or if you can't afford to redeem the property or continue making payments on it.

If you choose this option, you are not responsible for delivering the property to the creditor. They must make arrangements to get the property after your bankruptcy discharge is issued.

Too Broke For Bankruptcy

Pre-Bankruptcy Tasks

Before you take the steps to file bankruptcy, it's important to do some prep work to ensure the process goes smoothly. Here are the top things to do when you're preparing to file bankruptcy.

Task 1: Consider Switching Banks or Credit Unions

If you have a checking, savings, or other accounts at a bank or credit union you owe money to, when you file bankruptcy, they can (and likely will) freeze the funds and apply it to what you owe. Before you file bankruptcy, make sure you move your money to a bank or credit union you don't owe money to.

Switch all direct deposits to the new account and cancel automatic payments. Changing your bank account for direct deposits can sometimes take upwards of 60 days. Be sure everything is transferred to the new account before you file.

Task 2: Determine the Value of Your Assets

When you complete the required forms for bankruptcy, you'll need to know what property you own and how much it's worth. This includes your vehicles, property, jewelry, furniture, etc. Use the current value of your assets, or the "fair market value."

For most items, you can use the comparable sales price. Look at similar items for sale online or at thrift stores to see what they are selling for. Keep a log of where you looked or how you determined the value to support your valuation of your items.

For more valuable items, such as jewelry or art work, an appraisal may be a more accurate way to assess the value. This, however, isn't necessary for most household items.

Task 3: Complete the Required Credit Counseling

When you're ready to file bankruptcy, your first step is to complete credit counseling with an *approved* credit counseling agency. This must be done within **180 days** of filing bankruptcy. If you and your spouse are filing together, each of you must complete the required credit counseling before you file.

The credit counseling may be completed one-on-one, in a group, over the phone, or online. A list of approved credit counseling providers is available on the court's website: https://www.justice.gov/ust/list-credit-counseling-agencies-approved-pursuant-11-usc-111

Credit counseling agencies typically charge a small fee (from $0-$50) for their services. If your household income is less than 150 percent of the poverty level, you'll qualify for a fee waiver or a sliding scale fee.

Once you complete your credit counseling, you'll receive a certificate from the agency. Save this certificate and submit it with your bankruptcy filing.

Filing Chapter 7 Bankruptcy

Step 1: Decide How You'll Pay the Filing Fee

Although you don't have the expense of an attorney when you file bankruptcy by yourself, you'll still need to pay the required fees when you file. As of June 2018, this fee is $335.

If you can't afford to pay the $335, you have two options:
- Applying for a fee waiver.
- Applying to pay the fee in installments.

Bankruptcy Fee Waiver

To qualify for a fee waiver, you must be unable to afford to pay in installments and your family's income must be less than 150% of the official poverty guideline last published by the U.S. Department of Health and Human Services. For 2018, this is $3,137.50/month for a family of four. The full guidelines can be found online: http://www.uscourts.gov/sites/default/files/poverty-guidelines.pdf

To apply for a fee waiver, complete the Application to Have the Chapter 7 Filing Fee Waived (Official Form 103B) and submit it when you file bankruptcy.

Paying In Installments

If you cannot afford to pay the $335 in full, you can apply to pay the fee in installments. This will give you 120 days from when you file to pay the remaining balance.

To apply to pay the fee in installments, complete the Application for Individuals to Pay the Filing Fee in Installments (Official Form 103A) and submit it when you file bankruptcy.

Note: You will not receive a discharge until the fee is paid in full. If you fail to make the agreed payments, your case may be dismissed.

Step 2: Complete a Creditor Matrix

When you file bankruptcy, you must prepare and submit a mailing list called the creditor matrix. This is a list of creditors you owe money to. This mailing list contains all of your creditors' and their addresses. This information can also help you complete Schedules D and E/F. There are specific guidelines listed below that you must follow when creating your matrix.

Required Information

Your creditor matrix entry must contain the name and complete mailing address of each of your creditors and/or equity security holders. You're responsible for ensuring this information is complete and accurate before submitting it. If any changes need to be made after your creditor matrix has been submitted and filed, it can delay the process and the court may charge a fee for adding or deleting names and addresses.

Formatting Guidelines

Each bankruptcy court will have a different set of formatting guidelines and procedures for completing the creditor matrix. Contact your local bankruptcy court to determine what their requirements are: http://www.uscourts.gov/court-locator

Step 3: Complete the Required Forms

There are several forms you'll need to submit when you file Chapter 7 bankruptcy. Often, this is what stops most people from filing without an attorney. The forms are long and can get repetitive, but it's important to complete them all.

If you don't file the proper forms timely, your bankruptcy case may be dismissed. While some forms can be submitted within 14 days of filing bankruptcy, it's best to submit them all upfront to ensure your case proceeds smoothly.

For information on completing these forms, review the instructions published on the United State's Courts website: *http://www.uscourts.gov/sites/default/files/instructions_individuals_0.pdf*

Required Initial Forms

The filing fee is these forms are required to file Chapter 7 bankruptcy:
- Voluntary Petition for Individuals Filing for Bankruptcy (Official Form 101) http://www.uscourts.gov/file/22496/download.
- Statement About Your Social Security Numbers (Official Form 121) http://www.uscourts.gov/file/18787/download.

- If you cannot afford to pay the filing fee, complete and submit the:
    - Application for Individuals to Pay the Filing Fee in Installments (Official Form 103A) http://www.uscourts.gov/sites/default/files/form_b103b.pdf, or
    - Application to Have the Chapter 7 Filing Fee Waived (Official Form 103B) http://www.uscourts.gov/sites/default/files/form_b103a.pdf.
- The creditor matrix you completed earlier.

Additional required forms that may apply
If your landlord has an eviction judgement against you, also submit:
- Initial Statement About an Eviction Judgment Against You (Official Form 101A) http://www.uscourts.gov/sites/default/files/form_b101a_0.pdf, and
- Statement About Payment of an Eviction Judgment Against You (Official Form 101B) http://www.uscourts.gov/file/18708/download (If you want to stay in your rented residence for more than 30 days after you file for bankruptcy).

If you are using a bankruptcy petition preparer to type your forms, also submit:
- Bankruptcy Petition Preparer's Notice, Declaration, and Signature (Official Form 119) http://www.uscourts.gov/file/18785/download, and
- Disclosure of Compensation of Bankruptcy Petition Preparer (Form 2800) http://www.uscourts.gov/sites/default/files/form_b2800_0.pdf.

Required Forms To Be Filed Within 14 Days

When you file Chapter 7 bankruptcy without an attorney, these forms are required to be filed within 14 days, however, it's best to submit them when you file bankruptcy:

- Schedules of Assets and Liabilities (Official Form 106) including:
    - Declaration About an Individual Debtor's Schedules (Official Form 106Dec) http://www.uscourts.gov/sites/default/files/form_b106dec.pdf.
    - Summary of Your Assets and Liabilities and Certain Statistical Information (Official Form 106Sum) http://www.uscourts.gov/sites/default/files/form_b106sum.pdf.
    - Schedule A/B: Property (Official Form 106A/B) http://www.uscourts.gov/sites/default/files/form_b106ab.pdf.
    - Schedule C: The Property You Claim as Exempt (individuals) (Official Form 106C) http://www.uscourts.gov/sites/default/files/form_b_106c.pdf.
    - Schedule D: Creditors Who Have Claims Secured by Property (Official Form 106D) http://www.uscourts.gov/sites/default/files/form_b106d.pdf.
    - Schedule E/F: Creditors Who Have Unsecured Claims (Official Form 106E/F) http://www.uscourts.gov/sites/default/files/form_b106ef.pdf.
    - Schedule G: Executory Contracts and Unexpired Leases (Official Form 106G) http://www.uscourts.gov/sites/default/files/form_b106g.pdf.

- - Schedule H: Your Codebtors (Official Form 106H)
    http://www.uscourts.gov/sites/default/files/form_b106h.pdf.
  - Schedule I: Your Income (Official Form 106I)
    http://www.uscourts.gov/sites/default/files/form_b106i.pdf.
  - Schedule J: Your Expenses (Official Form 106J)
    http://www.uscourts.gov/sites/default/files/form_b106j.pdf.
  - Schedule J-2: Expenses for Separate Household of Debtor 2 (Official Form 106J-2) *Required only in certain circumstances. Review the guidelines on the form to determine whether you need to complete it*
    http://www.uscourts.gov/sites/default/files/form_b106j2.pdf.
- Statement of Financial Affairs for Individuals Filing for Bankruptcy (Official Form 107)
  http://www.uscourts.gov/sites/default/files/form_b_107.pdf.
- Statement of Intention for Individuals Filing Under Chapter 7 (Official Form 108)
  http://www.uscourts.gov/sites/default/files/form_b108.pdf.
- Chapter 7 Statement of Your Current Monthly Income (Official Form 122A-1)
  http://www.uscourts.gov/sites/default/files/form_b122a-1.pdf.
- If necessary, Chapter 7 Means Test Calculation (Official Form 122A-2) *If required based on Form 122A-1*

http://www.uscourts.gov/sites/default/files/form_b_122a-2.pdf.
- If necessary, Statement of Exemption from Presumption of Abuse Under § 707(b)(2) (Official Form 122A-1Supp) *If required based on Form 122A-1.* http://www.uscourts.gov/sites/default/files/form_b 122a-1supp.pdf.

You must also submit:
- The credit counseling certificate that you received.
- Copies of all payment advices (pay stubs) or other evidence of payment that you received within 60 days before you filed your bankruptcy case.*

*Some local courts may require that you submit these documents to the trustee assigned
to your case rather than filing them with the court. Check your local court's website to find out if local requirements apply.*

Step 4: Attend the Meeting of Creditors

After filing bankruptcy, you'll receive a notice with the date and location of your Meeting of Creditors, also known as the 341 hearing. This meeting will usually take place within 21 to 40 days of filing bankruptcy. During this meeting, you'll meet with your trustee and answer any questions they have.

In most cases, you will sit in a meeting room with other debtors until your name is called. When your called, you will approach the trustee's desk. Your meeting will likely be done within 5-10 minutes.

Although creditors can attend this meeting, they usually don't. You will be placed under oath and asked questions, such as "Is everything in your bankruptcy papers correct to the best of your knowledge?" and "Have you made any recent large payments to relatives or creditors?".

Make sure to bring photo ID, such as your driver's' license, and your social security card to the meeting. You'll also want to bring a copy of the bankruptcy forms you filed and any supporting documentation you were asked to bring. Your creditors will have 60 days from your Meeting of Creditors to object to discharge.

Step 5: Complete the Required Debtor Education Course

Before your bankruptcy case will be discharged, you must attend a debtor education course. The debtor education course may be completed one-on-one, in a group, over the phone, or online. A list of approved providers is available on the court's website: https://www.justice.gov/ust/list-approved-providers-personal-financial-management-instructional-courses-debtor-education

These agencies typically charge a small fee (from $0-$50) for their services. If your household income is less than 150 percent of the poverty level, you'll qualify for a fee waiver or a sliding scale fee.

Once you complete your debtor education course, you'll file Form 423 Certification About a Financial Management Course: http://www.uscourts.gov/sites/default/files/form_b423.pdf. This form must be filed **within 45 days** of your meeting of creditors.

Too Broke For Bankruptcy

Discharge and Beyond

At the end of your Chapter 7 bankruptcy case, you'll receive your bankruptcy discharge if you've completed all of the court's requirements. Usually discharge will happen within four months of filing bankruptcy. Once you've been discharged, you will receive the discharge order in the mail and a copy will be sent to your creditors and your bankruptcy trustee. Make sure you keep the discharge order in a safe place with your other bankruptcy paperwork.

After discharge, you'll be ready to start rebuilding your financial future. Your bankruptcy will stay on your credit report for 10 years from the date of filing, but don't let that scare you. Getting new credit lines and auto loans after bankruptcy isn't nearly as difficult as it's made out to be, although you may be looking at higher rates. Your credit score may even improve after discharge.

Going through bankruptcy gives you the opportunity for a fresh start. Without debt weighing you down, you can start focusing on saving money and building the future you want.

Glossary for Chapter 7 Bankruptcy

Annuity — A contract for the periodic payment of money to you, either for life or for a number of years.

Automatic Stay — An injunction that automatically stops lawsuits, foreclosures, garnishments, and all collection activity against the debtor the moment a bankruptcy petition is filed.

Bankruptcy petition — The document you file to open the bankruptcy case. (There are official forms for bankruptcy petitions.)

Claim — A creditor's right to payment, even if contingent, disputed, unliquidated, or unmatured.

Codebtor — A person or entity that may also be responsible for paying a claim against the debtor.

Collateral — Specific property subject to a lien from which a creditor may be paid ahead of other creditors without liens on that property. Includes a mortgage, security interest, judgment lien, statutory lien, or other lien.

Community property — A type of property ownership available in certain states for property owned by spouses and, in some instances, legal equivalents of spouses.

Community property states and territories include Arizona, California, Idaho, Louisiana, Nevada, New Mexico, Puerto Rico, Texas, Washington, and Wisconsin.

Consumer debt — A debt you incurred primarily for a personal, family, or household purpose.

Creditor matrix or mailing matrix — A list of names and addresses of all of your creditors, formatted as a mailing list according to instructions from the bankruptcy court in which you file.

Creditor — A person or organization to whom you owe money or who claims that you owe it money.

Current value or value — The amount property is worth, which may be more or less than when you purchased the property. Absent specific instruction, the value should be the price that could be realized from a cash sale or liquidation without duress within a reasonable time.

Dependent — A person who is economically dependent on you regardless of whether the person can be claimed as a dependent on your federal tax return. However, Chapter 7 Means Test Calculation (Official Form 122A-2) use the term in a more limited way.

Discharge — A discharge in bankruptcy relieves you after your bankruptcy case is over from having to pay debts that you owed before you filed your bankruptcy case. Most debts are covered by the discharge, but not all. Only your personal liability is removed by the discharge.

Disputed claim — A debt you do not agree that you owe. For instance, your claim is disputed if a bill collector demands payment for a bill you believe you already fully paid.

Exempt property — Property, or the value of a portion of it, that the law allows you to keep for your use rather than surrender it for the payment of your debts, provided that you
follow the correct procedure to claim the exemption.

Equity — The value of your interest in property that remains after liens and other creditors' interests are considered. (Example: If your house valued at $150,000 is subject to a $50,000 mortgage, there is $100,000 of equity.)

Fair Market Value — The price a willing seller and buyer under no pressure would agree the item is worth.

Garnishment — A procedure by which a creditor can reach money of yours that is in
the hands of a third party to satisfy a debt. Garnishments are sometimes used by creditors to obtain money from your wages or bank account.

Joint petition — One bankruptcy petition filed by a husband and wife together.

Judgment lien — A lien that arises as a result of a judgment against you.

Meeting of creditors — Also known as the 341 hearing. The meeting where you will meet the trustee appointed to your case to answer questions under oath. Creditors may show up, although this isn't typical for most cases.

No-asset case — A chapter 7 case where there are no assets available to satisfy any portion of the creditors' unsecured claims.

Non-dischargeable debt — A debt that cannot be eliminated in bankruptcy. Examples include a home mortgage, debts for alimony or child support, certain taxes, debts for most government funded or guaranteed educational loans or benefit overpayments, debts arising from death or personal injury caused by driving while intoxicated or under the influence of drugs, and debts for restitution or a criminal fine included in a sentence on the debtor's conviction of a crime. Some debts, such as debts for money or property obtained by false pretenses and debts for fraud or defalcation while acting in a fiduciary capacity may be declared nondischargeable only if a creditor timely files and prevails in a nondischargeability action.

Presumption of abuse — A rebuttable legal presumption that you have too much income after allowed expenses to be granted relief under chapter 7.

Property you own — Includes property you have purchased, even if you owe money on it, such as a home with a mortgage or an automobile with a lien.

Reaffirming a debt — Agreeing to repay a debt that would otherwise be discharged by entering into a new written agreement with the creditor. A reaffirmation agreement may allow you to keep property that a creditor has the right to take from you because it secures the debt being reaffirmed. For a reaffirmation agreement to be effective, there are many procedural and legal requirements that must be satisfied during the bankruptcy case.

Trustee — The bankruptcy trustee appointed to oversee and administer your case.

Unexpired lease — A lease that is in effect at the time you filed for bankruptcy.

Made in the USA
Monee, IL
04 January 2025